Machines We Use

IT'S SCIENCE!

Machines We Use

Sally Hewitt

CHILDREN'S PRESS®

A Division of Grolier Publishing

NEW YORK • LONDON • HONG KONG • SYDNEY
DANBURY, CONNECTICUT

© Franklin Watts 1997
First American edition 1998 by
Children's Press, A Division of Grolier Publishing
Sherman Turnpike, Danbury, CT 06816

Hewitt, Sally.
    Machines we use / Sally Hewitt
        p. cm. -- (It's science!)
    Includes index.
    Summary: Examines various simple machines and how they are used to
make work easier and provides activities using wheels, levers,
pulleys, screws, and more.
    ISBN 0-516-20793-8 (lib. bdg.)   0-516-26392-7 (pbk.)
    1. Machines--Juvenile literature.   2. Machines--Experiments-
-Juvenile literature. [1. Simple machines.] I. Title.
II. Series: Hewitt, Sally. It's science!
It's science!
QC73.4.H49 1997
621.8'11--DC21   97-2154
                                                                          CIP
                                                                           AC

Series editor: Rachel Cooke
Art director: Robert Walster
Designer: Mo Choy
Picture research: Sarah Snashall
Consultant: Sally Nankivell-Aston
Photography: Ray Moller unless otherwise acknowledged

Printed in Malaysia
Photographic acknowledgments:
Eye Ubiquitous p. 15
Michelin Tyre Public Limited Company cover & pp. 10/11
Zefa p. 19 top left
The publishers would like to thank the following for their help with the items in this book:
NES Arnold Limited pp. 5, 12, 22;
Tridias, 6 Bennett Street, Bath BA1 2QP 01225 314730 pp. 23, 27.
Thank you, too, to our models: Henry Moller, Wilfred Cross, Jordan Hardley, Ken King, Lauren
Shoota and James Moller.

Contents

Rolling Along

A log and a block of wood are different shapes. The log is a cylinder and the block of wood is a cube.

A log will roll along when you **push** it, but when you push a block of wood, it will only slide.

🖐 TRY IT OUT!

Find a cardboard roll and a box like these.
Which one is a cylinder like the log?
Which one is a cube like the block of wood?

Make a slope with a book or a piece of cardboard.
Try rolling the box and the cardboard roll down the slope.
What happens?

A cylinder is a good shape for rolling.
We can use a cylinder to help us get **jobs** done.

A rolling pin and a paint roller are both cylinders.
What jobs do they help us to do?

TRY IT OUT!

Try **pulling** a wooden block along the
floor. Can you feel it slide?

Now try pulling it along over
a row of felt tip pens.
Can you feel it roll?

Is it easier to slide or to roll things along?

7

Machines

A **machine** is something we use to make **work** easier.

Scissors, a knife and fork, a whisk, and a shovel are all simple machines. What jobs do they make easier?

What would it be like if you tried to do those jobs without using anything to help you? Could you dig the garden without a shovel?

TRY IT OUT!

Try to make a paper circle without using scissors to help you. Now cut out a circle using scissors. What differences do you notice between the two circles?

A washing machine, a calculator, and an iron are much more complicated machines.

Could someone wash clothes, do mathematics, and iron the creases out of clothes without using these machines?

Which one of these machines only needs to be switched on and then does its job by itself?

Wheels

Wheels are shaped like a circle.
They are a good shape for rolling along.

Wheels have to turn round on a rod.
The rod is called an **axle**.

axle

 TRY IT OUT!

Cut out a circle from thick oaktag and make a hole in the middle of it for the axle.

Push a piece of drinking straw through the hole you have made.

You can fix the axle to a box like the one in the picture to make a wheelbarrow.

Could you fix the wheel to the box so that it turns without an axle?

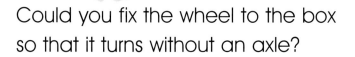

Some of these wheels are for rolling along.
Which of these wheels have got other jobs to do?

Look around you when you walk down the street and spot all the things that roll along on wheels.

LOOK AGAIN

Look again at page 6 to find another shape that is good for rolling.

Would a cylinder be a good shape for a wheel?

11

Wheels with Teeth!

handle

The teeth around the edge of this wheel are called **cogs**.

A wheel with cogs can be used to turn another wheel with cogs.

When the yellow handle is turned, the small red wheel goes round.

Can you see how the cogs on the small wheel make all the other wheels turn round?

These machines have wheels with cogs that make them go round and round.

Your feet push the bicycle pedals round and round. The pedals turn small wheels with cogs round and round. The small wheels turn the bicycle wheels round and round.

Can you see how the small wheels are linked together?

Can you tell which parts of this watch go round and round?

Pulleys

This suitcase is too heavy for Ben to lift up without some help. A special machine called a **pulley** can help him to lift it.

A pulley is made up of a rope that runs around one or more wheels.

The suitcase is fixed to a pulley wheel with a short rope. Another long rope goes around the first pulley wheel and up and round a second one. Ben is pulling down on the other end of the long rope. Can he lift the suitcase up now?

The pulley wheels make the job easier.

The more pulley wheels there are, the easier it is to lift heavy loads.

This crane is lifting an enormous piece of machinery.

How many pulley wheels can you spot?

 **THINK ABOUT IT!**

How is a pulley shaped to hold the rope? Could you use a cylinder for a pulley?

Levers

Levers are another kind of machine that help to make a job easier.

The screwdriver and the hammer are being used as levers to lift something up.

When the end of the screwdriver is pushed down it will lift up the lid of the can.

What will the hammer lift when it is pulled down?

In order to work, a lever must turn around something. The part it turns around is called the **fulcrum**.

 TRY IT OUT!

Find a strong ruler to make a lever, a wooden block, and some books. Try lifting the books on the end of the ruler. What happens?

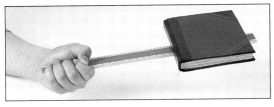

Now put the brick under the middle of the ruler to make a fulcrum. Try lifting the books with the ruler again.

The books are easier to lift now the ruler is moving around the block. You are using the ruler as a lever.

17

More Levers

A wheelbarrow is a different kind of lever that we use to make it easier to lift a heavy load.

The heavy load that needs to be lifted is the pile of leaves. Can you see that the load is in the middle of the lever?

LOOK AGAIN

Look at all the levers on page 16. Is the load that needs to be lifted in the middle or at one end of each of the levers there?

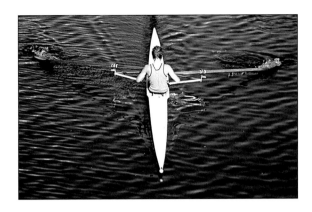

Oars are levers too. When you pull on one end of the oar, the other end pushes through the water and moves the boat along.

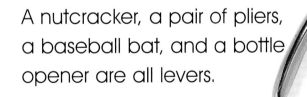

A nutcracker, a pair of pliers, a baseball bat, and a bottle opener are all levers.

What job does each one do? What part of the lever do you hold? Do you pull, push, squeeze, or **swing** the lever to get the job done?

19

Hinges

Hinges are a special kind of lever. They join two things together but still let them bend and move.

Did you know that hinges join some of the bones in your body together?

 TRY IT OUT!

Bend your knees. Bend your elbows. Open and shut your mouth. Can you feel the hinges in your elbows, your knees, and your jaw letting your bones bend and move?

Imagine what would happen if your bones were all firmly fixed together and not joined with hinges!

Hinges are used to fasten things together that have to open, shut, and fold.

A door opens and shuts on hinges. Try pushing a door open near the hinges. Now try pushing it near the handle. Which is easier?

 **TRY IT OUT!**

You can use very simple hinges to make models.
Bend a rectangle of oaktag in half.
Glue the oaktag on to the two pieces of your model that you want to stick together.
Make sure your hinge is free to bend along the fold.

Balancing

Jessie and Ben are **balancing** on the seesaw because they are both about the same **weight**.

The apples are balancing on the **scales** because they both weigh the same.

What would happen to the seesaw if Dad was on one end and Ben was on the other?

What would happen to the scales if a leaf was in one pan and a stone was in the other?

All kinds of things use balance to help them to work properly.

The flour in the pan is balancing with the weights on the other side of the kitchen scales.

The elephants on this mobile hang evenly because they have been carefully balanced.

The cook has used a 2 lb weight. How much flour has she put on the scales?

What would happen if this large elephant was swapped with a smaller one on the mobile?

 THINK ABOUT IT!

A balance is another type of lever. Where are the fulcrums on the seesaw and the kitchen scales?

Slopes and Screws

Paul can push along a heavy load of earth in a wheelbarrow.

He has made a **slope** with a plank to help him to push the load up the step. How could he get the load up the step without the slope to help him?

A slope is a kind of simple machine that makes lifting a heavy load easier.

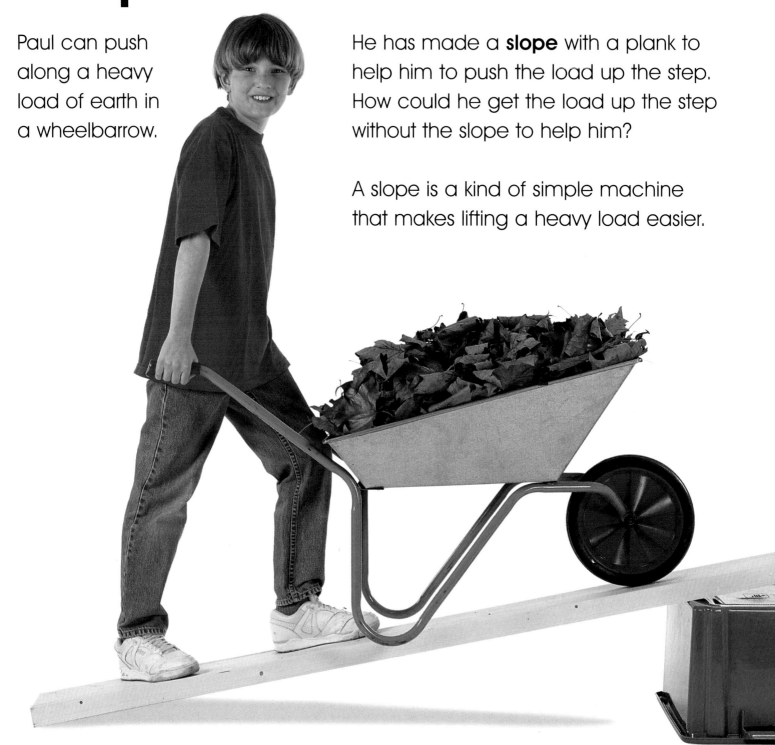

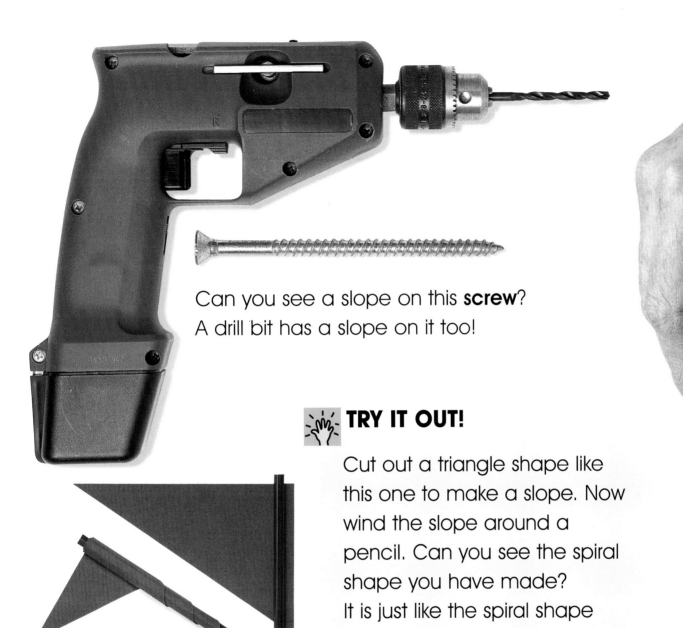

Can you see a slope on this **screw**?
A drill bit has a slope on it too!

🖐 TRY IT OUT!

Cut out a triangle shape like this one to make a slope. Now wind the slope around a pencil. Can you see the spiral shape you have made?
It is just like the spiral shape round the screw and drill bit.

The slope that winds round the screw helps to force it into the wood. When you turn the screw round and round, the wood moves up the slope. This pulls the screw little by little into the wood.

25

Making things go

This metal **spring** is shaped like a spiral. If you squash it down, it will spring back into shape when you let it go.

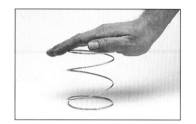

 TRY IT OUT!

Fold a strip of oaktag backwards and forwards. Tape the end down and squash down the top. Let it go and watch the oaktag spring back up. You can use a spring like this to make a pop-up card.

Tie each end of a long piece of string to the ends of a long wooden block. Twist the block round and round until the string is wound up tightly. Let the block go and watch it turn round and round as the string unwinds.

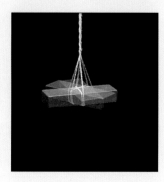

How would you make this toy go?

When the key is turned, it winds up tightly a metal coil inside the toy. As the coil unwinds, it moves the toy along.

All machines need something to make them go.

Can you spot something that needs to be switched on?
What needs to be wound up to make it go?
What needs a spring to make it go?
What needs someone to work hard to make it go?

LOOK AGAIN

Look at all the different machines in the book. Can you tell what makes each one go?

Useful Words

Axle An axle is a rod that goes through the center of a wheel. A wheel turns around on an axle.

Balancing When two objects that weigh the same amount are put on scales, the scales are balancing. If one object is heavier, it will make the scales go down on one side.

Cog A cog is one of the teeth found round the edge of a cog wheel.

Fulcrum A fulcrum is the fixed point or edge a lever turns around.

Hinge A hinge joins two things together but still lets them move. Hinges attach a door to its frame but still let it open and close.

Job A job is work that has to be done.

Lever A lever is a bar that turns around a fixed point. Levers can help to make a job easier to do.

Machine A machine is something we use to make a job easier.

Pull People and machines can pull. An engine on a train pulls carriages along. When we pull something, it usually moves towards us.

Pulley A pulley is a machine made of ropes and wheels. It makes it easier to lift heavy loads.

Push People and machines can push. A bulldozer pushes earth out of the way. When we push something, it moves away from us.

Scales Scales are machines that measure how much things weigh.

Screw A screw is a simple machine. It is a cylinder shape with a slope wound around it.

Slope A slope is like a gentle hill. Slopes can be used as simple machines. It is easier to walk or push things up a gentle slope than up a steep hill.

Spring A spring is a piece of wire that has been coiled round and round. When you stretch it or squash it down and then let it go, it springs back into shape again.

Swing Something that is hanging down, like a swing in a park, will swing backwards and forwards when it is pushed. Some levers swing around their fulcrum.

Weight You can find out how heavy an object is by measuring its weight. The weight of an object can be measured on weighing scales.

Wheel A wheel is a circular-shaped machine that helps us do a job. Wheels turn round on axles.

Work Work is done when something is moved or stopped. People and machines can both do work.

Index

About this book

Children are natural scientists. They learn by touching and feeling, noticing, asking questions and trying things out for themselves. The books in the It's Science! series are designed for the way children learn. Familiar objects are used as starting points for further learning. Machines we use starts with a rolling log and explores simple machines.

Each double page spread introduces a new topic, such as levers. Information is given, questions asked and activities suggested that encourage children to make discoveries and develop new ideas for themselves.
Look out for these panels throughout the book:

TRY IT OUT! indicates a simple activity, using safe materials, that proves or explores a point.
THINK ABOUT IT! indicates a question inspired by the information on the page but which points the reader to areas not covered by the book.
LOOK AGAIN introduces a cross-referencing activity which links themes and facts through the book.

Encourage children not to take the familiar world for granted. Point things out, ask questions and enjoy making scientific discoveries together.